FIRST STEPS

*Poemwalking
the Ice Age National Scenic Trail
in the Northern Kettle Moraine*

Katrina Serwe

Brain Mill Press
Green Bay, Wisconsin

Some of the poems in this collection first appeared in the following publications and are reprinted here with permission:

ArtAsPoetryAsArt 2024: "What I Can't Change"
Bramble Lit Mag: "Poemwalking"
Portage Magazine: "Backtracking" and "Life Isn't Always Green"
Scrawl Place: "Misfit"
The Solitary Plover: "Hepatica Stars"
The Wisconsin Fellowship of Poets 2023 Triad Contest, theme (What Would Have, Could Have, Should Have Been If...), Honorable Mention: "Perspective"
The Wisconsin Fellowship of Poets 2023 Triad Contest—Kay Saunders Memorial Emerging Poet, 3rd Place: "Ephemeral"
The Wisconsin Fellowship of Poets, 2025 Wisconsin Poets' Calendar: "Fly Song"

Copyright © 2025 by Katrina Serwe.
All rights reserved.

Published in the United States by Brain Mill Press.
Print ISBN 978-1-948559-90-4
EPUB ISBN 978-1-948559-91-1

Cover photograph © Katrina Serwe, 2025.

www.brainmillpress.com

FIRST STEPS

First Steps was a winner of the 2024 Brain Mill Press + Wisconsin Fellowship of Poets Chapbook Contest.

for those who make the trail possible

Ice Age Trail Volunteers

I see you—
in the mowed grass,
fresh yellow trail-blazes,
that new-wood smell
across the bridge
as my dry feet follow
mapped-out clear
views on this thread
of connection we call
the Ice Age Trail.
I whisper my thanks
to you—my friends
whose names
I may never know.

The Ice Age National Scenic Trail

CONTENTS

POEM	ICE AGE TRAIL SEGMENT	
What I Can't Change	Milwaukee River Washington County	1
The Weight We Carry	Parnell	2
Hepatica Stars	Greenbush	3
Where I Go for Comfort	Kewaskum	4
In the Summer Haze	South Kewaskum	6
When Calm Comes	Parnell	7
MisFit	Cedar Lakes	8
Out of Place	Slinger	9
Backtracking	Pike Lake	10
Fly Song	Milwaukee River Washington County	12
Detachment	Pike Lake	13
Life Isn't Always Green	West Bend	14
Strange Dreams	Holy Hill	16
Warm Welcome	Milwaukee River Washington County	18
Perspective	Loew Lake	19
Water	Greenbush	20
Contradictions Coming Together	Greenbush	21
Unruly	Undisclosed	22
Reverberations	LaBudde Creek	23
Early Spring	Parnell	24
Waking Up	Parnell	26
Ephemeral	Parnell	27
Walking There and Back	Milwaukee River Fond du Lac County	28
Poemwalking		29

About the Author   31

FIRST STEPS

What I Can't Change

The bones of this place are the same.
Familiar silty soil under my feet—
rock, sand, and clay piled in moraines
rolling between forest and meadow,
kettle ponds guarded by mosquito buzz.

I smell the cool of sun-dappled green
as I hold thick maple girth in my arms.
It is as still as I want to be. Glaciers
shaped this land 10,000 years ago
and I want another 10,000 without change

but I feel the shifting sand under my feet
where the river is carving a new bend.
Every breeze transforms the day
with comfort or distress. In the end
it doesn't matter if I stay or go—

so I begin my journey of a thousand miles.

The Weight We Carry

My sister and I climb the stairs to view
the question mark shaped lake.

Color pushes up the hillside through
the brown wake of winter, ephemeral

violet purple, hepatica blue, trillium white.
Overhead, calls to disperse from flock and pair:

sandhill cranes, red-winged blackbirds, geese.
They are looking for their own space to create

this year's new, which my sister doesn't see
as she rails against luck and life and lack

until her energy fades and knee aches
and my concern turns to fear.

I leave her to rest, shoulder my pack
and quicken my pace to return

to the parking lot. Try not to admire
twisted roots upturned to the sky,

mushrooms that look like rocks and rocks
that look like mushrooms, feel the lightness

of my stride across the marsh, up flowered
hillsides. Relief is outlined in Chevrolet red.

I climb into my efforts to rescue,
fasten my seatbelt to pick her up, find her

sitting folded in on herself
next to a boulder.

Hepatica Stars

on the backs of hummocky hills
folding over and into each other
we push through yesterday's dry leaves
to seek our time in the sun, cast our
yellow-centered stars across a palette
of brown as we open our centers
to warmth, stretch skyward, propagate
our creativity in shades of lavender,
violet, plum, galaxy blue … our time
to bloom long as an April day before
the rush of spring is over and we are
consumed by tomorrow's green tide

Where I Go for Comfort

it starts where the barn sits tall,
faded to the color of cedar waxwings

who are feasting in scrubby juniper
watching the baked-grass trail

give way to cool hardwoods rooted
in stony hills filled with echoes

of bird song, cicada hum, woodpecker
taps, hickory nuts falling

on mossy tumbled rock walls that released
glacial-grit farmland back to forest, turns

to borrowed path across a cut wheat field
and deer-tracked fence line where

clouded sulphur butterflies drink
from alfalfa purple and red clover

crops of sandhill cranes stand
reminders of generosity, leisure and honey

at the ski hill and apiary where landowners
make space for uninterrupted trail, boardwalk

through marsh funneled under highway
to splash into meadow

pink and yellow with coneflowers,
cottonwood trees and swallows

sweep the sky, changing perceptions
in this summer jumble of life

where the monarch casts a shadow
as large as the crow

In the Summer Haze

Ridge, Townhall, Wildwood
roads to travel with views
into other lives—
garage doors and windows
open to August-humid air

two little boys on bikes
zig and zag past an old farmer
who lifts a square-bale his own size
and a woman in a blue-print dress
bends to weed a row of beans

cars pass with a wave,
a cardinal sings red from
the power line before
road turns to grass-trail
crowded thick with summer

green—grapevine climbing
over sumac to a cool
maple-woods welcome,
offering an extra loop of trail
for a moment longer to linger

in the shade before a new
wood-bridge crosses the marsh,
follows the soybean row to end
at the sheet-metal grain elevator—
space held for unripe crops

When Calm Comes

Clouds heavy and low—the barometric
pressure over my head, the atmosphere I know
is not welcome to steps I take regardless
into this forest I want to know and follow
into the dark shadow of pine boughs. I find
Little Mud Lake reflecting the stony sky.
Twin stumps cut for sitting beckon rest
but this calm won't last. I feel the weight

of air shift as crows call, rain drops, slow
then faster, wind whips needles, flash then
splitting thunder
                crash
                        of primal fear
                                down my spine

or is it a thrill at nature's hidden power,
a truth revealed? The sky shifts with the last
drops of rain through sunshine, aspen shiver
wind-breath relief. I move forward on soft-
sand footing, my tension somewhat lessened
after the sky has fallen.

MisFit

Alongside the traffic hum,
two fawns eat from the farmhouse garden
with its budding six-tree apple orchard.

The smaller one with brighter
spots steps forward, wondering—
what other tamed wild-thing lingers

on wide-shoulder gravel? I walk
five miles to enter the woods
at Polk Kames, moraine-peaks grounded

in tall, old oaks and thick maples.
Today they are lush, with full ponds
and hungry, swathing me in relentless mosquito hum.

I hurry to find
road edge again where the breeze
frees the itch from my skin.

Trading one hum for another,
I cannot decide
which I like better.

Out of Place

I trade my backpack for a purse
and follow trail-marking yellow blazes hidden
beneath streetlights, 2-hour parking
and railroad signs—a scavenger hunt
through other people's neighborhoods,
feeling awkward as the handwriting

recording my steps, my thoughts,
a pause. The local crows call out
warning—but it's not for me.
They are chasing a hawk
from their forest-edge nests
at the end of Howard Drive.

I follow wooded cornfield edges,
cross the roar of Highway 60,
take my purse on connecting country
roads to Pike Lake trails, past backpacker
sites where I wonder what it would feel like
to through hike, until my stomach growls

and I turn to head back to the comforts
of town for coffee and a maple Pershing.
Where my purse will fit in, but my dreams
of big-pack long hikes will not and I
wonder how I became so good
at feeling out of place.

Backtracking

The yellow blaze forks.
I don't understand the choice.
This is a non-loop trail.
The ribbon of black and green
garter snake shares the sunshine
with me as I consult the map.

It is and it isn't a loop trail—
it can be if you want.
I choose the tower view of wind-
sculpted lake in gray marble,
splashes of vermilion on green
like the first raindrops of fall.

I follow a path I walked in spring
when I was filled with anger, fighting
against a world that no longer made sense,
struggling to problem solve the impossible,
seeking action to hide grief.
The trees here wear yellow sashes—

warning, the hillside is eroding, leaf
rot oozes from earth's torn flesh.
I feel it here, the shredded black edges
of grief, waiting for me like an old pack
left unshouldered until I regained
my strength to pick it back up.

I put it on like a shadow
heavy as a black hole, it pulls
warm wet streaks down my face.
I turn back on my tracks and climb
the tower a second time because I can.
I am alone and there is no one

to complain about the extra steps.
The clouds thicken and the wind grows
cooler. The weather is changing.

Fly Song

July flies orbit my head,
a hundred buzzing thoughts
in my favorite stretch of forest.
The faster I walk the more
they multiply—until I stop

and we listen to my breath
and birdsong, through leaves
playing in air, watch sunlight
scatter in the still understory.

I stand, the flies resume
their orbit. I don't know what
it means. Why is birdsong
beautiful and fly song
maddening?

Glacial grit slides
under my feet, sweat soaks
through my sundress.
At the green hand pump

I let iron-flavored water spill
into my thirst, find the gift
of striped brown and white
turkey feather, laughing
swipe it through my cloud of flies.

Ask it, what is the difference
between the song
of the bird and the fly?
It answers,
        Nothing.

Detachment

Morning-damp dirt trail
twists through green sumac
tipped orange-red.

Through the quiet, I hear
the sludge of worries I carry.
My steps slow through a thick

muck of fabricated responsibility—
the need to fix someone else
to cover my own pain.

In the thought rut of what I can't
change, I don't see the branch
fallen across the path.

A cardinal fires out—
pew, pew, pew ... be here now!
I exhale, focus my eyes, observe

cumulus clouds
over a goldenrod field splashed
with purple aster. I listen

aspen leaves clatter,
a thousand tiny hands
clapping.

Life Isn't Always Green

I've left Friendly Drive,
the car parked by the elevator.
My feet seek steps of solitude
and organic green life.

Traffic sound follows me, buzzing
through Kettle Moraine rocky ups
and downs like simmering anxious
thoughts. The noise, the humanness

I can't escape. Looking for beauty
I see brown, twisted, broken trunks—
their struggle to climb ended.
Trail moves from thinning trees to town.

Walking to Culver's, hope of wildness
dissolves like lemon ice down
my throat, but reemerges
in the park as city sounds

dissipate in unbroken brown water
around the feet of Ridge Run hills
where the path shifts, a result
of collective rerouting

around a wind-weeded branch
returned to feed the forest floor.
My thoughts settle on white ruffles
over brown decay—the fungi-coated limb

holding beginnings
      and endings intermingled
           gently forcing
    this new path.

Strange Dreams

Leaning into the greener
side of September
squirrels hurry to gather
black walnuts to tuck
away for comfort
on a colder day.
Twisting through
patchwork fields—
corn, clover, alfalfa,
trail is cooled
by tree-line shade
and vast blue breeze.
It dives into the arms
of a tall maple forest
riding a terminal moraine
to marsh traversed
by wooden bridge,
past fields of lime-green
dragonflies hunting
over golding soybeans.
Twin cathedral spires
peak from the canopy
on top of Holy Hill.
Here trees wear name
tags: oak, aspen, box elder;
wind stirs leafy daydreams
from rest at kame-top views.

The cathedral presides
over every opening—
closer, farther, closer
trail circles and moves
away from spires that linger
in furthering views.
A reminder that dreams
as strange as a hilltop
cathedral deep in a glacial
shaped forest can be
realized.

Warm Welcome

Seeking oxygen and birdsong—
balm that has eased countless worries,

I begin from a new spot—
air soft and bee balm spicy-sweet,

calm after last night's storm,
heating in the sun until I'm swimming

through humid green breath
of shagbark hickory, maple, oak,

heart-leafed basswood, quaking aspen
whispering stories of surviving, gathering

strength, drinking deep in the soggy hills.
I let the muted warm light lull me,

follow their dappled haze-shade across hogbacks,
down valleys, into daydreams rooted

in glacial grit, startle to find myself
so quickly in a familiar place.

Perspective

Switchbacks down green moraine
offer a cool welcome
on a summer-dressed fall day.

The immensity of the ridge
is something I can't understand
until the distance is traveled

when I can look back over
the bright where the meadow holds
space for knowing.

Water

its preciousness realized
when every drop is carried
and spilt equals thirst,
the consequences of actions
felt, a blessed lesson
of the earth—
I savor each drop

Contradictions Coming Together

Moving my feet   to rest my mind,

I walk in cloudless blue-   sky swept by violent wind,

inhale pine-fragrance   bled from logging cuts,

startle at the crack of tree-limb   falling through sunshine,

watch the orange-brown butterfly   rest on coyote dung,

admire the leaves of a seedling maple   emerging from a nursery of stones

and sparkles of amethyst hepatica   on old leaf-brown hillsides.

Looking for privacy in an outhouse, I laugh at two seat holes side-by-side.

Unruly

I like to pee in the woods
off the edge of the trail,
hidden behind a tree
      like a wild thing

squat low and hear
spatter on dry leaves,
watering the forest floor
      part of the hydrologic cycle

look around at tiny trees
reaching for the light,
green growing things
      whose names I want to know

listen for footsteps and
savor the thought of doing
something as old as humans
      harmless, yet illegal

Reverberations

I didn't know I felt the buzz of cars chasing circles on a track,
like the buzz of thoughts chasing circles in my mind. A buzz
that reverberated from Road America across fields, open roads,
miles of woods. Driving their buzz into the forest like a swarm
of mosquitoes. Pebbled dirt rolled under my feet as I climbed
mapled moraine seeking solitude. Continued up the next
and when it wasn't there, the next—until I forgot. I didn't realize
how my breath echoed the race, echoed shallow drafts of looping
noise, echoed reverberations from someplace else until
               it stopped.

Now tension in my chest exhausts
itself into a deep green

silence of tall pine
and cedar-fringe. I exhale

into marsh spilling out
under boardwalk—water

sparkles sunshine I'm first
noticing. I listen to my feet

drum the bleached boards—
realize I need the forest quiet

to find a rhythm outside
the track of someone

else's race.

Early Spring

I leave my excuses at home
and hike into the gray day.

Imprint my muddy footprints
on others and know I'm not alone.

The shapes of things stand
out on a monochromatic day:

crisscrossing humpback hills,
tree spines overlapping, some

windblown bent, others jagged-
edge split from storms,

their roots seeking ground
among moss-crusted boulders.

My thoughts stand out too,
storm-worn and anxious

until a cloud of field sparrows
sings them back to the present.

A hawk meets me at eye level
at the top of Parnell Esker.

We watch black ice sinking
into the skin of Butler Lake

as wind ripples with a knife-
edge of winter cold

and feel the stirring of our
blood already spring-warm.

Waking Up

The wind blows strong on a
cerulean day between spring rains.

Last year's beech leaves hang,
tattered lace in the understory.

The trees sway and squeak
as they wake to send sap to buds.

Crushed green ferns free themselves
from tired snow, reach up for the light.

Were they there all winter? Like me,
waiting for the wind to push them

through the cold
to welcome a new season.

Ephemeral

It is that kind of blue-sky day
when the salamander's tail

starts to dry ten steps from the mud.
The brown-winged butterfly

sails over a crust of snowbank
through the spring peepers' love-drunk calls

and the forest starts to push up green
through last year's brown.

I pick up the salamander, feel
dew-drop-cool feet wander

over my palm, shift my hands
for his gentle descent to new

wet grass at the shady edge
of the swollen marsh.

Walking There and Back

I skitter through leaf litter like a squirrel, follow
the intuition of a red fox across the road to the shelter

of the forest, pause to pluck poetry from the green
leaves of my mind, hear bird chatter through

the treetops, see church spires and question
why we imagine that a source of creation

would dwell indoors. My pack lightens
as my thirst deepens. I turn back, taking

a faster pace against the setting sun, follow
a cooler breeze into the mirrored view

where the tree shadows fall longer on the pond
and find the church obscured by moraine-top maples.

To know a place, I must see it both ways—
the different views of there and back.

I hear four bells by New Fane, another church
hidden from view and laugh at redundancy

echoing back across my steps, necessary
for the return home, I keep walking.

Poemwalking

I forget about the half-written story,
    the hopeful to-do list on my calendar,
        how long the backyard grass has grown,
            the unwashed dishes…

and follow curiosity down the curve
    of a hill, eager to discover what's around the bend—
        the shiver of aspen or thick pine-shade?
           I scratch my fingertips on goldenrod lace,

turn to see if the skittering squirrel is red, gray, or black,
    ponder the marsh, the still stench of purification,
        listen to crows call each other home,
           wait for the swallowtail to pause his thirst for nectar.

I look for the spaces of overlap—
    where water meets land,
        when hills stretch out to plain,
           how sunshine turns to shade

and see my thoughts change
    with the terrain, as I scribble
        in my notebook to catch
           the poem of my walk, to reflect
              back on another day.

About the Author

Katrina Serwe, PhD, worked as a therapist, professor, and researcher in the field of occupational therapy for over two decades. She started writing poetry after a transcendent midlife crisis brought her back to her love of literature, art, and nature. Her poems have been featured in a variety of publications such as *The Solitary Plover, Blue Heron Review, Bramble, Portage Magazine,* and *Scrawl Place.* Serwe was the first-place winner of the 2024 Wisconsin Writers Association Jade Ring contest for poetry. Her current project is foraging poems on Wisconsin's Ice Age National Scenic Trail. You can follow her journey at www.katrinaserwe.com.

www.ingramcontent.com/pod-product-compliance
Lightning Source LLC
Chambersburg PA
CBHW052127070526
44586CB00016B/2125